PERIPHERAL VISION

ALSO BY SUSAN KINSOLVING

The White Eyelash
Dailies & Rushes
Among Flowers

PERIPHERAL VISION

poems

Susan Kinsolving

Red Hen Press | *Pasadena, CA*

Library of Congress Cataloging-in-Publication Data

Names: Kinsolving, Susan, author.
Title: Peripheral vision : poems / Susan Kinsolving.
Description: First edition. | Pasadena, CA : Red Hen Press, 2018.
Identifiers: LCCN 2018043559| ISBN 9781597096157 | ISBN 1597096156
Classification: LCC PS3561.I578 A6 2018 | DDC 811/.54—dc23
LC record available at https://lccn.loc.gov/2018043559

The National Endowment for the Arts, the Los Angeles County Arts Commission, the Ahmanson Foundation, the Dwight Stuart Youth Fund, the Max Factor Family Foundation, the Pasadena Tournament of Roses Foundation, the Pasadena Arts & Culture Commission and the City of Pasadena Cultural Affairs Division, the City of Los Angeles Department of Cultural Affairs, the Audrey & Sydney Irmas Charitable Foundation, the Kinder Morgan Foundation, the Meta & George Rosenberg Foundation, the Allergan Foundation, and the Riordan Foundation partially support Red Hen Press.

First Edition
Published by Red Hen Press
www.redhen.org

ACKNOWLEDGMENTS

My appreciation to the editors of the following journals where some of these poems first appeared:

Caduceus, Chautauqua Review, The Common, Connecticut Review, Dogwood, Dos Passos Review, Light, Narrative, The New Criterion, The New York Times Book Review, Poetry Repairs, Rattle, Resurgence, Southwest Review, Texas Review, Tulips, Women's Voices for Change, and the anthology *A Ritual To Read Together: Poems in Conversation with William Stafford.*

For research regarding prosthetic eyes, I owe thanks to David Carlson, Anne Fadiman, Minh Farrow, Dr. David Gougelman, Ellen Clair Lamb, Elizabeth MacDonald, Pirie MacDonald, Jocelyne Rotily, David Scronce, Wendy Shay, Gayle Williams, and William O. Walker.

Articles by Katherine Ott, Frances Richard, Anthony Lydgate, and the Veterans Administration were helpful.

For the generous gifts of time and trust, my gratitude to:

Carol Franc Buck
Carol Muske-Dukes
Laura Baudo Sillerman
Reba & Dave Williams
Ucross Foundation, Wyoming
Tyrone Guthrie Centre, Ireland

For Richard Howard

CONTENTS

PERIPHERAL VISION

TRUTH BE KNOWN

ON SPINDRIFT DRIVE ONE NIGHT

A thirty-five-foot wave crashed through the house,
smashing windows, pushing a pillar into the ceiling,
and sweeping the desk out to sea where, strewn with kelp,
it floated away to rewrite that nightmare into a dream.

Years have washed over the details of my timely
escape from that rocky precipice on which I lived.
Yet I often yearn to retrieve one book,
an unabridged dictionary, a grand old Webster's

Second. Sometimes, I picture it still in the salt
water, all 2,289 pages rippling and disintegrating,
a plankton of syllables, drifting from pronunciation
and redefining each entry as food for fish.

Perhaps that is how the book will be returned
to me, on a platter of protein, bone, and etymology.
I would eat it with exactitude, separating the skin
and skeleton, one meaning from the meat

of another. I am but a beachcomber, pocketing
sand dollars, broken shells, hoping for a phrase.
I envy the ocean's endless lexicon, nameless
derivations, fluencies, unfathomable piracies.

MILLIONS

Half her head plays Lotto; the other half plays Emily
in *Our Town* or Amherst. By the synaptic second, re-
evaluations, generations of money, chicken coops and
attaché cases, markdowns and night shifts, lost, ex-

changed in a day. Even an orchard becomes her rapid
transfer system. Bees humming through stock quotes,
fruit infected with a taste of metal, clouds evaporating.
There's no accounting for it, the currency of time

on the take. In foreign countries she clutches her purse;
at home she forgets where she left it, behind a sofa
pillow or under a kitchen counter. But today an indigo
bunting takes her breath away while a real estate sign

puts its stake in the heart of the matter. She knows it
all goes someday. Maybe the sooner, the better.
A dry eye doesn't cry. What luxury to see a rare bird,
flown in flash, blue into blue, air to nowhere. How it goes . . .

AFTER FROST

As the poet said, I weep for what little things could make me glad:
those days perfected under the pines with Pamela, a mansion
in a rickety playhouse, daily dramas among three dolls, a feast
in a basket and her docile collie nudging with his long wet nose.

When autumn winds blew through her fields, oceans appeared.
Then we stumbled ashore to rediscover old cow skulls,
mossy and gray; their hollow eyes fixed on our eager fascination.
We named that ghostly land "The Bones Estate" and unearthed

its many treasures of rusted lanterns, broken bottles, bricks,
and shards of crockery. Each recovered relic was put to quixotic use.
A nickel established our lifelong wealth and a pair of bent glasses
framed our spectacular future. Now the years have made me sad

and simple. I turn to memory like an old beggar, but time is tight-
fisted, tossing a two-bit reverie onto the pavement of a cold day.

A DISTANCE

Audible but incomprehensible, friends speak from a distance.
She cannot grasp any meaning, even a water glass. Less is present,
more past. Milkweed makes sense of the autumn air, taking future
from here to there, nowhere. A flock of starlings settles its frenzy
in a field of wild asters. Her own hand could be gentler than God's.

TO HER IN HOLLYWOOD

I will not say goodbye to you, young actress
centered on your celluloid stage. Part of you
wants me to wave a fond farewell, release you
from your parental past, abandon you to film,

fate, and future. But no such luck, my darling
daughter. Put a continent between us and still
I will call, as if to a wrong number, awaiting
cursory forgiveness. Someday, I'll be at your

door like a weary salesman hoping for a hint
of engagement. The tough truth of our invisible
matter is just this: I will depart from you only
when I am dust. And even then, you may sense

me swirling with your triumphs or settling
sadly over surfaces when you are forlorn.
I simply cannot say goodbye to you, even
when, at wit's end, I'd almost like to.

COMING TOWARD ME

She's four years old with her hands on her hips
and elbows flared, to emphasize the interrogative.

"Hong Kong's the city, King Kong's the monkey,
right?" I nod, right. She smiles with self-

satisfaction, having sorted the Kongs correctly.
Soon she'll be on to bigger stuff, the difficult

differentiations: appearance versus reality,
irony or coincidence, shades of truth, white lies.

Parent as predicate will end, my answers just
unwanted advice. The only hope is not to end

like an old movie with airplanes circling the city,
evolved animals being killed; shots, screams, sirens

sorting out crises of an apocalyptic world. And I,
useless for any affirmation, will be liable as a ghost.

PAGE COUNT

I was reading a big book. When my mother lifted it
with both hands, she exclaimed, "You're reading *this*?"
Surprised, I smiled, anticipating an exchange of ideas
and intimacies, a different dialogue from the usual.
The book's title was *An Embarrassment of Riches*,
about Dutch culture in the Golden Age, but it was of no
consequence. My mother set the volume down to ask,
"Just what do you think that thing weighs? Five pounds?
More?" I thought of Emily Dickinson writing, "My mother
does not care for thought," and I said, "Less, much less."

REMODELING

Like many new houses in the fifties,
hers featured a shoulder-high room divider
for plants, a leafy look-through between
the front hall and their deadly living room.

One afternoon, with a sledgehammer
and crowbar, her mother bashed away
at that divider until only broken boards,
dirt, and uprooted plants remained.

When her father returned, the mother stood,
hammer in hand, triumphant. "What the hell's
going on in here?" he said, dropping his briefcase.
Silent, her mother slowly smiled, a warning

of further wreckage. At age ten, she knew
all parents' rooms were somehow divided;
many mothers wanted to tear every damn house
apart. But no one spoke a word. Like a trance

and a truce, in slow motion, her father mixed
a martini while the mother put wilting plants
in water. Quietly, they cleaned up the mess
and later at a nice restaurant, enjoyed supper.

The week after, her mother took a pickaxe
to the father's car. His affair with a "Born-
Again Bimbo" had gone too far. His check-
book was the paper trail, verifying betrayal.

"FILL THE CAVITY WITH CRUMBS"

We were divorcing, but after giving Thanks-
giving. It was all relative with relatives. Every-
one came wanting: to grate, mash, carve, or
strain. It was a strain. Who knew a frozen

turkey took three days to thaw? We hauled
boiling water to the bathtub. Fowl was
the noun, but quickly became adjectival.
My almost-ex overcooked cranberries until

they exploded across his shirt like a machine gun,
proving him the victim. The garbage disposal
jammed and overflowed as his cousin waltzed in
with her special dish, lurid whipped yams, dotted

with mini-marshmallows in a heart shape around
a big smiley face. I eyed the mace. Uncle Ed said
an ecumenical grace. Drunk, Aunt Dede described
her sister's firm grasp of the superficial, then

added, make this insult official. My mother
replied, I won't cry. Because someday I'm going
to die. After a long pause, eight people said
they'd have to skip the pie and say an early

goodbye. Dad called it mincing the mince.
Quite undone, he laughed alone at his pun.
For me, the day seemed endlessly long. But I
was thankful nothing had really gone wrong.

"NEVER WRITE ABOUT ME AGAIN"

That's my ex shouting from his cell, ricocheting
off a tower into my reddening ear. "Listen,"
he yells, "Do you hear? Nothing in that poem is
true. It's only your point of view. Keep this up
and I swear I'll sue." A static pause. "What if,"
I ask with a quiver, "it's not about you? But another,
a recent ex, who was quite a lover?" Cupid-like,
I shoot that stinging shaft into his head. Two clicks.
The phone goes dead. Once again, enough said.

COMMINGLING

As directed, Mother's ashes were "released"
into Lake Michigan. Fresh water, no salt tears,
and a continent between her ashes and Father's

which were to be "scattered with dignity"
into the Pacific. For him, I was asked to sign
a release not to bring a lawsuit in case *commingling*

occurred in the crematorium. "There's nothing
he'd like more," I laughed. "Hot women were always
in his mix. And now I'm left to give permission?

Well hell, I'll pay extra to give him a party!
Put him in with a fiery redhead and an ash blonde.
He's a Navy man, going into an unknown ocean."

THE WINTRY ONE

for Liam

Haltingly, I described doors frozen shut,
windows etched with ice, abundant snow,
how no one could come or go. He smiled
so I admitted my happiness at being alone
for days in an old farmhouse, isolation
its own sensation, a kind of celebration.

"I guess you're a misanthrope," he said,
hurling back my snowball of sentiment
just as I had shaped it, but harder-packed.
It hit the right side of my head; crystals fell
past my collar, down to my breast. I shivered.
I was his conquest. Hot, cold, self-confessed.

NYMPHAEA

The second I saw water lilies under ice,
I knew we too were trapped by time.
The grand botanical garden would grow
as it had for centuries, without our being
or blossoming, romance or regret. Strange
to think that spring would thaw those
extravagant white blooms into extinction,
turn cold encasement to warm decay.
How artful we were in not advancing
that image beyond the moment, keeping
ourselves captivated all afternoon.

REFLECTIONS ON NARCISSUS

Remember years ago, a day among our last,
when we kept digging in the bed
though it was cold and overcast? Half-

smiling, *What might it mean*, you asked,
*that I'm burying King Alfreds while yours are
called Bronze Queen?* I gave a shrug

as you went on, *Pliny said these bulbs
drug, make the body numb. He called Ovid's myth
merely "meddlesome."* A long silence ensued.

You shoved your spade along a string
of naturalizing lines. I stomped clumps
into the ground and skewed our spring designs.

Echo died, I finally replied. *Her curse was endless
naming, yet Narcissus saw himself clearly past
all blaming.* Why after decades do I bring this

nonsense back? Perhaps the mind is like an old
bulb sack with dark words waiting to have their
say. But when I see yellow waves upon the hill

or a pitcher full of bright jonquils, I feel an old
dismay. For we disguised our poison
as these flowers do in their clear viscosity

and buried love so deep, we never realized
its luminosity. When we parted, I wandered lonely
as a cloud, looking for you in any crowd.

PERIPHERALS

HER MANIFEST METAPHORS

To assuage my sixteen-year-old student
that I will not betray her lyrical intimacy,
I suggest there is solace in suicidal songs,
relief in such searing reverie, referring to

"the speaker" while scrupulously avoiding
"you." Thus, we continue our solemn literary
appreciation of self-destruction. No madness
in our method, only clanging church bells,

sanitarium chatter, physics of space, and
heartsick matter. Together we leap from our
separate balconies, swim past the horizon,
swing from our own imagistic ropes, count

syllables as pills, acknowledging each artful
ledge, each enjambment's razor edge. This:
our chosen form, so much denial to teach,
so many closures erased, edited, reeducated.

MATHEMATICAL DREAMS

Mathematical dreams are never mine.
The brain is its own narrow bed.

On my pillow, a cello never plays,
a scalpel never slices through surgery,
beehives are untended. What images

come to the worried seamstress,
weary mountaineer, hopeful soldier,
anxious accountant, contented wrestler?

Who sees ancient Greece or tropical
fish undulating past, a diving bell ringing?
Why is there not total otherness in sleep?

The opera singer snoozing beside an engineer,
their dreams so distant with heads so near.

THE FASHION OF LA FOLIE

She insisted that a gazebo, grotto, and gate be added
to the Estate. Two obelisks were next. And soon, a sham
castle was built on adjoining land. Then she planned

a Greek temple for a statuesque Aphrodite and six
water-spouting nymphs. Plus, a pagoda! Her follies
were, as Lord Clark said, *monuments to mood*. But

she had so many! Her fortune fed her fantasies until
one stormy day, she was caught in a downpour. Under
the rubble-stone roof of her hidden hermitage for hours,

she waited, her peasant costume sopping, her doeskin
slippers soaked. The cracking sound was not thunder.
Mossy timbers crashed on her coifed head. Found

dead, she was soon entombed in a mausoleum. In time,
vandals destroyed the weeping angels, Corinthian capitals,
and garlanded urns. Her resting place in ruins, a final folly.

NIGHT SIGHT

To attain acute night sight, a person needs
two hours in the dark. Photons trip rod cells
into action. Three scientists proved this by
working with a toad and a suction-electrode.

Night sight takes a lifetime to attain. Wandering
in snow on moonless nights is only a start. Grey-
scale, as it's called, will expand between extremes,
archetypes, dark and light, with every implication.

Acute night sight is an inescapable howling
in the head, a bellowing in the brain, so much
becomes lurid in the dark: nocturnal animals,
enraged insomniacs, death wishes under heaven.

TWELVE SHELVES

Eager to please, we prepared the house for her long-
awaited visit. To make shelf space, we boxed our books.
Then we unpacked her china, stood amid piles of bubble
wrap and tissue paper, arranging the display, staging her
collection. Imari plates of mandarin orange were propped
upright on little wooden easels and kept at a distance from

Coalport cobalt blue. Spode platters were positioned around
a Royal Crown Derby tea set. Limoges were gathered into
thematic groupings. We were sure that she would be thrilled
to see her treasures from the past so prized in the present.
But when the presentation came, she glanced without interest
or recollection, then wandered past the shelves to a window.

PERIAPT AND HU-KWA

She bought the tea trolley at auction along with other pieces
that took her fancy, mostly chinoiserie. After the diagnosis,
she placed the trolley in the living room where chemo
and chamomile often kept her asleep on a chaise. One day,

longing for distraction, she began to dust and noticed a small
oblong compartment underneath the trolley: a secret drawer,
stuffed with tissues. One little tug at the wad revealed a gold charm
bracelet, its trinkets depicting a charmed life: a ruby-studded heart,

a champagne bottle, the Eiffel Tower, two terriers, shamrock,
mortar board, horseshoe, and a zodiac medallion: the Cancer sign.
After recovery, when she served high tea off the trolley, her bracelet
jangled and clinked against the china: a new charm for every year.

A LASTING LEGACY IN WARSAW

Decades had passed, but still she could conjure up a fury
at the thought of her mother's will. How her sisters had
received china, silver, and jewelry. Her only inheritance
was an old armoire. When retrieving a garment, she often
banged the doors shut in anger. Eventually, the back panel
cracked; nails came loose. One day, she glimpsed a bit
of paper, the edge of a five hundred thousand note.
Behind the panel, there were thousands more, taped
in tight imbricated rows, a fortune once, but now
brittle, beige, worthless, defunct. Irony and memory
became her currency, her exchange, her reevaluation.

CONSPIRATORS

With his lookout, a wide-eyed child,
he shared the mischief of his cane,
its stealth encased in wood and glass.

The girl waited for that secret time
when the long diagonal was raised
to his lips, the liquor pouring

from that secret tube, down his throat.
During those furtive gulps, her duty
kept her in high spirits, always inviting

the chance of being caught with brandy
in the air and his brass knob unscrewed,
the horsehead half-hidden in her hand.

PARLIAMENT PASSES THE INCLOSING LANDS ACT, 1809

The open-field system would end. Every acre was enumerated
in a way John Clare could not comprehend. Why should footpaths
have fences, streams be made straight, why fell trees, wall a field
and lock it with a gate? No longer could he drink from Eastwell spring;
the bubbling water was penned by scaffolding. *No Trespassing*

at every turn, posted over scurvy-grass, loosestrife, vetch,
clover, and fern. Clare doffed his cap and wept for his right to roam;
in chicory, thistle, briony and buttercup, he'd always been at home.
Or coming upon a gypsy camp (fires and tambourines!) he'd share
his fleabane, borage, parsley, some beans. Again the labouring-class

had lost to the well-to-do, those new proprietors of blackberry, hemp-
nettle, toadflax, and meadow rue. Clare questioned his sanity, fearing
a familiar hell, but tramped on to say his farewell to mallow, teasel,
oxlip, and pimpernel. He knew this ramble was one of his last; every
field, farm, and forest would be enclosed. The open world was past.

FROM THE WINDOWS OF THE
KEW LUNATIC ASYLUM

The view excavated any hope of escape. "Ha ha!"
the trench, that sunken fence, seemed to say
with its furrows dug deep enough for despair.

Though from the other side, the public saw
swept views, open expanses, a landscaped guise.
The asylum appeared to be a place of liberty!

But between normalcy and its aberrant
neighbor, conduits had been cut to demoralize
the committed while reassuring the rest.

No common ground was shared between
that haha outside and the hysteria within.
Those chasms were created to confine each

breach that behavior had transgressed.

UNNUMBERED

Her fame merited the dawn, so
I drove to beat the crowds
through the new light of New England
to be first in Amherst.

I thought it luck, my parking space
so near The Homestead door—
then rushed to gain admittance
to her chambered site—

'Twas there my ardent pace stopped
as insight held me still,
I dwelt *alone* with poetry
as she, despite her will.

THE END IN SIGHT

In an old elemental elegance, Oliver imagined
a starry night. I am not so bright, settling
for wind in the trees or a snowfall's solace.

For Peter, mirrors covered, no comfy chairs.
He watched shiva through a window once,
seeing his own ghost. My mother wanted

swing music, a return to the forties when
she could move, look fabulous, and laugh.
Maybe everyone should have some swing.

How awful for others, the ones left yearning
for only an hour resembling peace, or at long
last, just something filling, satisfying, to eat.

BLACK HILLS BY DAY

Time has been a wild horse, twirling leaf, startled mirror.
But there, where the river slowed, my hand was taken by water.
So many birds have flown into eternity while I have been
absorbed with anxiety, allowing the light to fail without a look.
I have intruded on the sanctity of grief. I have been absent
at the birth of change. For one day in Wyoming, I was able
to stay alone in astonishment. Prairie grasses leaned. Large
animals stood near. Clouds reshaped mountains. The wind
spoke in an ancient voice. I wanted nothing, but more time.

HISTORY OF A METAPHOR

GLASS EYES

*And yet: what other body part could conceivably be
substituted in glass?* —Frances Richard

The man with the glass leg could not take a step

for fear of cracking. The woman with the glass tongue

could not taste soup or ice for fear of shattering.

The child with the glass ear could not risk

the rock band or the symphony. The man

with the glass nose would look silly; his sinuses

showing, his nostrils transparently blowing.

The girl with the glass heart would have a broken

heart, never to mend. And how far could one go

with a glass toe? A glass finger would break

in a simple handshake. Glass genitals would not

be fun once all the smashing had begun. No, only

glass eyes will do, looking alive while utterly untrue.

THE OCULARIST SAID

"A convincing eye comes from attention to detail:
the sunbursts or striations of an individual iris,
or those unique specks of color that appear to be
just dropped in, dabs of interest, as if an artist
took an arbitrary brush over the palette. Ah, those
dark brown eyes flecked with amber, those blue
eyes shaded violet, the green ones edged in russet.

The surrounding sclera too has its tints, white
with subtle shades of yellow age, grey illness, or
the pink of drink. This is why an off-the-shelf eye
looks fake, hokey, and hackneyed. So sit down,
please. Try not to blink. In order to paint your eye
I need to think about color and you. Now I must
stare at your one eye while you gaze at my two."

THE EFFECT ON ELIZABETH

Seeing the situation of wearing
a glass eye as strikingly similar
to that of writing poetry, the difficulty
of combining the real with what is
decidedly unreal, natural with

unnatural, Bishop observed her
grandmother's glass eye. In Rio
in the sixties, she described that image,
the curious effect of producing what
looks to be normal, yet is artificial,

a thing synthetic yet insightful—
the glass eye, blindness being beheld.
And upon reflection, one can further
speculate: imagine a sighted eye
seeing itself, glass in a mirror.

PICTURE THIS

Like the hairdresser, manicurist, or tattoo artist,
the ocularist accommodates eccentric requests.
A fan of the Tennessee Vols wants his eye colored
orange with a capital "T" where the pupil should be.

Another man fancies his Harley, as if the tiny image
could cycle through his head, bike around his brain,
then speed back again, a wheeling dot revving,
swerving, and braking in his socket parking lot.

Another wishes his false eye to be an insignia for
the Marine Corps, his living eye sacrificed in war.
A blinded Turk asks for a star and crescent moon;
a chubby gourmand wants a fork crossing a spoon.

Portraits are complex tasks, a face within a face,
a miniature mask. One woman wants her accident
recreated; she'll wear a target with an arrow. A bird-
watcher wants a minikin egg, nest, and sparrow.

Smiley faces are still a craze, a cartoon to counter
every frown, unless of course, it's worn upside-down.
A teenager thinks that a fist with a middle finger thrust
might be a shock. An old man wants a surrealist clock.

The list is long, full of surprises: an Eiffel Tower, golf ball,
iridescent daisy. The ocularist accepts any challenge, no
matter how crazy. He recalls his silver dime, details worthy
of a counterfeiter, or the iris made of cubic zirconia for

maximum glitter. He mentions semiotics, how "a sign
denotes identity, idiosyncrasy, symbols of the so-called
'real me.' But we see ourselves as others seldom do.
In that way," laughs the ocularist, "a false eye is true."

HOW IT HAPPENS

How it happens is always horrific. How, without other eyes,
could it be otherwise? In the 1820s, one town in England
reported eight losses. First, a cinder flew from a fireplace
into a cradled infant's eye. Days later, across the lane, a stone-
cutter's chisel shot loose a shard. Then there was a young boy

breaking coal with a rock; the black fleck could barely be
seen beside his own dark pupil. When wheat chaff
went from the sickle blade to stick in the ciliary muscle
of a man hurrying his harvest before a rainfall, the town
grew superstitious. The assorted afflictions evidenced

an omnipotent overseer, one who did not like what he
was seeing. The fifth incident was an avenging whiplash
over a team of obstinate oxen; a backlash whipped
across the driver's eye. The oxen remained unmoved
after the flagellant switch. That evening the driver's

distraught wife stooped quickly, without looking, over
the spool holder of her spinning wheel. Her scream and
resounding blasphemies convinced the town that such
coincidence was a curse. Quickly, they congregated
at the church to pray. Mercifully, their winter went

without an ocular event. But on the first spring day,
two more mishaps darkened all optimism. A lilac
branch gashed a girl's retina, then a bumblebee
caught in a boy's eyelashes stung his cornea.
The priest, in his most extreme visions, never thought

sin would be so evident and perfectly punished.
He sermonized that all the single-eyed sinners must
repent, and he pictured for them an awaiting hell.
Then he implied that tithing might restore lost vision,
and he kept close watch out of the corner of his eye.

THERMAL DYNAMICS

In 1840, Herr Baumann, half blind, but overheated
with hope, bought a beautifully crafted glass globe
from a famed German master specializing in "eyes
light as bubbles and thin as skin." The hollow orb,
fragile as a Christmas ornament, was custom painted
to match the actual eye. The master claimed that
an eye socket never sagged under such insubstantial
weight, a lid could close with comfort and a handsome
countenance could reappear as if unaltered by injury.
He promised Baumann's disfigurement would be
dispossessed. And so it was until one snow-blind night,
leaving a sweltering café, Baumann took a step into
the full force of freezing air. Instantly, the orb imploded,
shattering and leaving slivers lodged in the tissue
of his empty eye. Does this anecdote mystify, mortify?
Is it a tale of artifice, agony, or irony? Is it another
black patch of history or scientific probability?

HELEN KELLER IN THE NEWS
(1880–1968)

At age eleven, when she made a mistake, she was accused
of plagiarism, of being "a living lie" for writing of violets,
mist, clouds, and woe, her ultimate verbal conceit: a rainbow!
But Helen triumphed with a poet's best refute. The mind's eye,
she told those myopic men, is imagination. She was resolute that
words and images came from the brain; they were selfsame.
Twenty years later, reporters would rhapsodize over her "big wide-
open blue eyes." How they could "magnetize, animate, and gaze
with such a seemingly seeing glance." Eyes that "almost dance
with delight as if they had normal sight!" Eyes "so lively, luminous,
and bright!" The press published those hyperboles, unsuspecting
of any vanity from a woman who could not hear or see. Yet,
Helen had a secret. Such beauty came from surgery. Her big, blue,
idealized eyes were acrylic. The public never knew her trick.

AMBROISE PARÉ, 1579

A war surgeon, he saw all losses: life being
the larger part; limbs the lesser. Legs hanging
from trees; on the field, hands disarmed.
Teeth missing; toes afloat in a bucket of blood.

A competent carpenter, he sawed and drilled,
pulled with pliers, hammered and hacked.
Much symmetry was skewed, gaps and gapes,
the glaring absence of an eye, gouged

and gone, bulging on the tip of a bayonet
or staring up from the ground, its final site.
Paré didn't like the look of it; being French,
he began to paint. On tiny metal discs, covered

with chamois, he made the marks of a pupil
and soon became an artisan, attending to the iris
and its color wheel. A cord was tied around
each patient's head to keep the enameled artifice

in place. Paré called his creation an *Ekblepharon*,
eked from the Greek. He also sculpted hands and feet,
bringing such pieces to the maimed men, offering his eyes
as a new point of view, an ultimate *trompe l'oeil*.

PROSTHETIC ANECDOTES

THE CASE OF THE CARROT

They made the news, the local couple and their lawsuit.
The verdict came down: intent. He'd "hurled a raw carrot"
during an argument; the orange root hit her right eye-
ball, rupturing it. He was in handcuffs, sorry-looking

as she showed the jury her prosthetic eye, removing it
from her head to hold in her hand. She said, "See
what he did to me?" Astonished, the twelve stared:
an eye was looking back at them from the palm

of her hand. In defense, the husband pleaded, "I
didn't 'hurl' a mallet or a carving knife. Just a carrot.
Vegetables aren't meant to harm. In fact, carrots are
supposedly good for the eyes." A mistake, to have

joked. The jury turned against him, and Justice,
wearing a blindfold in order to weigh evidence
without prejudice, let the acrylic eye tip her scale.
Indicted by a carrot, he served two years in jail.

EVIL EYES

Back from Athens, she arrived at her Lake Forest estate
with a bag full of presents for the help: piles of glass
pendants, discs of blue and white concentric circles
hanging from silken cords and silver chains. An evil eye
for each. Maids, butlers, and cooks had never seen

evil eyes in Illinois. They feigned gratitude, regretting
she bestowed trinkets instead of tips. Then she read
aloud from a printed card, explaining the eye was meant
to deflect envy and its invidious consequence. But
pronouncing *apotropaic*, she realized her mistake:

she'd reversed the talisman's presumed protection. The help
needed no shield against envy from others. *She* was
the envied one; and now, without a safeguard, she stood help-
less in front of her servants. The ones who eyed her excesses
every day were watching her anew, keeping evil in hand.

FRANKIE MINH

In the Vietnamese orphanage, her eyes became infected;
without anesthesia, they were gouged out, in order
to rid the place of germs. At age five, she was adopted
by an American actress and renamed to honor Sinatra.

On the school playground, with her black eye patches,
Frankie learned to play the pirate. When she was given
her prostheses, she hid them like plundered treasures
among her dolls and socks. Keeping acrylic eyes in her

sockets was not, to her mind, a good place to put them.
Her dread was doll-like, that having glass eyes would
empty her head. But once, at a grand house party full
of adult celebrities, she wore the eyes. When one fell out

and into a bowl of caviar, kindly laughter filled her ears.
She was the center of attention, a star. After the eye was
washed off, she held it in her hand, perceiving its elusive
charm and how clearly she could be the life of the party.

SECOND GRADE, SEAVIEW ELEMENTARY SCHOOL

When Anna Rose O'Keefe's acrylic eye popped
out of her right orbital socket and rolled across
the linoleum floor, the class went crazy, wilder
than the day the lizard got loose or the time
Tiffany Arguelles threw up her grape Jell-O.

The eye ended up under Aaron Kagan's chair
and he was terrified to touch it. The teacher too
looked stricken; his classroom was out of control,
with squeals and shrieks probably reaching
the principal's office. So he shouted for quiet,

then told Anna to retrieve her eye. "Prosthesis,"
she corrected, proud of pronouncing the word.
The teacher told her to sit in the hall. So there
Anna sat, holding her acrylic eye in her hand
like a talisman. She resisted being sad, smiled

instead, glad about all the wild fun. Besides,
she thought the teacher was dumb: he knew
nothing about bone mass, tissue structure, or
reconstructive surgery. Quietly, Anna began
to sing:

I'm wild eyeless rose.
I'm the sweetest flow'r that grows.
You may search ev'rywhere,
but none can compare.
I'm the wild eyeless rose . . .

ON ISLA NEGRA

Maria Celeste is crying again, tears
caused by condensation. Her melancholy
is made of wood, carved into her ironic
smile. She was Neruda's best figurehead,
a garland crowning her polished hair,
an oaken arm on her hip, as if ready
to scold his delayed return. Years ago,
his famous green ink dried. But no
matter, she still leans toward his chair
though the resident of earth will never
reappear. He who feared the ocean
entered the unfathomable. How strange
that he is gone and she remains, exile
of the sea, housed in his maritime hoard,
glassy-eyed, as the tourists stream past.

PVT. WILLIAM O. WALKER RECALLS

Walter Reed Army Hospital:
Eye, Ear, & Nose Unit, 1947

motto: *We Provide Warrior Care*

The war was over. The only thing to kill was time.
And memory. Looking in a mirror, a GI wondered
why. Whether to laugh or cry, he had to face his
future with a new face, one that would be recomposed
with an acrylic eye, a rubber ear, a grafted nostril,
or a plastic nose. *Pretend it's camouflage*, the surgeon
said. *And thank the Lieutenant Colonel you're not dead.*

The Army took pride in its reconstructive surgery
and prosthetic ophthalmology. Still, the wounded
had to wait through weeks of boredom and healing,
though nothing dulled what they were feeling. Best
to keep the bandages and badinage going; dark
humor was vital to prevent grief from showing:
shouts of *Hey, Buddy, I hear you're here for an ear!*

And *Watch out, One-Eye's gonna cry!* They yucked it
up because deep down, they knew they were forever
fucked up. As if their faces weren't freakish enough,
all prostheses were also on display. Case after case,
day after day, the GIs could see their bits of misery,
exhibited under glass and labeled: Ears come in six
skin tones. And there were piles of soft plastic ears

in white, tan, brown, black, yellow, and a sickly grey.
Creepier than taxidermy, one man said, eyeing the eyes,
a huge glassy array of colorful striations, like marbles
left from a huge schoolyard shoot. Hundreds of them,
precious juvenile loot, suggested games and mischief,
ways of ending monotony, a bit of fun for an amputee.
(Boys will be boys, even when they're maimed men.)

First, they crooned to the female nurses during rounds:
Lucky, lucky you! You've got two!
Two eyes and two breasts! Fair and square.
One's for the Army; you keep the spare!
Then a nurse would find a rubber nose floating
in a bedpan. Or prosthetic ears fitted over toes. Or
covering a Private's nose. A glass eye in a navel

was a shock. *(Keeping an eye on the Navy!)* A male nurse
glimpsed one in a buttock. The eye peeked out between two
hairy cheeks. *Surprise! I'm watching you! I'm the asshole*
with a view! The nurses knew the men were bored and
felt like freaks, confronting mirrors when they did,
facing an aberration who was once a baby, a kid, a lover,
someone's son. So the prosthetic jokes were just therapy

and good fun; while piece by piece, the display cases
were undone. For poker, the guys needed chips, so they
took a pile of plastic eyes, which made the game come
alive. *Raise you five.* Then on the table rolled five
blue eyes, with a face value of a buck. Cards continued,
but with luck, another game was played in the showers.
The ante was upped when an acrylic eye fell on the floor.

In the suds, find the eye! . . . And while you're down there,
give it try. How 'bout opening my other eye! And so they
bonded, fought time, and survived, trying not to feel
too queer about missing half a nose, an eye, or an ear.
The toys with which they played were all grotesque,
but isn't war, when at its best? Like trading tin soldiers
for body parts? Or eyes for medals, those purple hearts?

L'OEIL DE VERRE

On the Mediterranean, between Marseille
and Cassis, are the Calanques,
French fjords, famous for their ocher cliffs,
deep water, and rugged beauty.

Just below the precipice of one
is a hollow, a huge geological gouge,
as if a protrusion of earth fell
into the sea, leaving a glaring cavity.

For centuries, fishermen have seen
this site change from a rocky concave
to a glassy convex: a shimmering eyeball
bulging from the inlet wall.

This metamorphosis
from aperture to eye
is explained as a mix of reflective
minerals with refracting mists.

But this answer seldom satisfies anyone
who has seen that strange vision:
the lost eye, returned to its socket,
staring from its height, fixed on the sea.

One can only wonder if the earth
watched the world emerge,
observed ancient fishing boats,
old sails of commerce, pleasure cruises

from centuries past, and the ships
of countless wars. Perhaps the planet lost
its sight, the original eye eviscerated,
overwhelmed with global extremes.

Now that the gods are gone,
the oceans depleted, the air
heated with particles, we are left
to witness our illusions, past

and present. We envision an overseer,
a glass eye forged from shattered
quartz and splintered light. Inevitably,
it is blindness we cannot see.

L'OEIL-BALLON
"The Eye Like a Strange Balloon Mounts Toward Infinity"

Over the flat land with vaguely distant mountains
and indistinct stalks of grass, the inflated envelope
appears suspended. Who can tell if the gaseous air
is bringing that big ball up or down? Odilon Redon
drew an eyeball on the balloon, charcoal iris, and eye-
lashes looking up. Up, even if going down. Below,
many netted lines hold the observation platform,
that perplexing dome. Is it half a head, cut off
at the nose? Only Redon knows. Best to let it go
with the airflow, see a floating Cyclops observing
the sky, his aerated eye unblinking, yet winking.

BIOGRAPHICAL NOTE

Susan Kinsolving was born in Illinois, raised in New England, and educated in California. She has taught at the Bennington Writing Seminars, Southampton College, Willard-Cybulski Correctional Institute, University of Connecticut, California Institute of the Arts, and Keystone Academy in Beijing, China. She has received poetry fellowships from France, Ireland, Italy, Scotland, Switzerland, New York, Illinois, and Wyoming. As a librettist, she has heard her works performed in New York, California, Italy, and the Netherlands. She is Poet-in-Residence at the Hotchkiss School in Connecticut.